"Like its predecessor, this elegant collection of poems touched my spirit. It will join *Mala of the Heart* in the exam room of my internal medicine office, gently reminding my patients that love is the answer."

— KATHERINE L. CHICK, MD

"Love is the means and the end. Love is the medium and the message. Love honors *self* and love honors *other*; love points to where these are distinct as well as to that even vaster plane where they are in common. That's what Ravi Nathwani and Kate Vogt convey to us here. Best of all, here everything and everyone are invited. In an age of boundaries being frantically drawn and redrawn in the name of self-preservation, this book lovingly reminds us of the boundless."

— BJ MILLER, executive director of the Zen Hospice Project

"With an incredibly varied assortment of authors and poetic forms, this collection wraps the heart in words of comfort, joy, wonder, and the many faces of love. Each page is an invitation to explore who, how, and why we love and how to express it in so many beautiful ways. Congratulations to the creators of *Mala of Love* for offering us this compilation, and congratulations to all of us, the readers, for our new access to luminous poems as a resource for inspiration and reflection."

— DAVID LUREY, international yoga teacher, musician, and founder of the Global Bhakti Project

"Ravi Nathwani and Kate Vogt have put together an utterly ravishing book of love poems — a slim volume that reverberates with the mysteries of the human heart. It will live now, permanently, next to my bed — to soothe my mind and heart with both the memory and the anticipation of love."

— STEPHEN COPE, senior scholar in residence at Kripalu Center for Yoga and Health and author of *The Great Work of Your Life*

MALA
OF
LOVE

MALA
OF
LOVE

108 Luminous Poems

Edited by Ravi Nathwani & Kate Vogt

Contributing Editor, Soleil Nathwani

New World Library
Novato, California

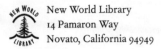 New World Library
14 Pamaron Way
Novato, California 94949

Text design by Tona Pearce Myers

Library of Congress Cataloging-in-Publication Data
Names: Nathwani, Ravi, [date] editor. | Vogt, Kate, [date] editor. | Nathwani, Soleil, contributor.
Title: Mala of love : 108 luminous poems / edited by Ravi Nathwani and Kate Vogt ; with contributions from Soleil Nathwani.
Description: Novato, California : New World Library, [2016] | Includes bibliographical references and index.
Identifiers: LCCN 2015041157| ISBN 9781608684106 (hardback) | ISBN 9781608684113 (ebook)
Subjects: LCSH: Love poetry. | Religious poetry. | BISAC: POETRY / Inspirational & Religious. | FAMILY & RELATIONSHIPS / Love & Romance. | RELIGION / Spirituality.
Classification: LCC PN6110.L6 M25 2016 | DDC 808.81/9354—dc23
LC record available at http://lccn.loc.gov/2015041157

First printing, February 2016
ISBN 978-1-60868-410-6
Printed in Canada on 100% postconsumer-waste recycled paper

10   9   8   7   6   5   4   3   2   1

INTRODUCTION

Look
what happens to the scale
when love
holds
it.

It
stops
working.

— KABIR

IN A FEW SIMPLE WORDS, Kabir invites us to step into the balance and grace of love. When we acknowledge the presence of such love in our lives, our awareness expands and our fears recede. We are uplifted and — even if momentarily — we notice the harmonious flow of nature around us. The air seems lighter, and we feel suspended in unending joy and gratitude.

When we pause and truly *look*, as Kabir suggests, we realize that love is not a commodity to be earned or bartered for. It is inherent in everything, weaving us all together. Like the sky holding the clouds, love doesn't grasp or cling to us; it just patiently holds us. And, as in Kabir's imagery of the scale, love doesn't erase the world. Instead, it is the doorway within that world to infinite peace and calmness.

Sages and saints have long told us of the sweet, gentle ocean of love. We are never separate from this love, yet in our clouded view we see ourselves as single drops in the ocean, separate from the other drops and the ocean itself. We are bound by self-absorption, longing to connect with all the other drops. We forget that love is so all-pervasive that even *we* are love. Every thought, every action, every memory — no matter where our human mind places it on the scale of good to bad — is love.

As long as we believe we are different drops in the ocean, the light of love will refract differently. We speak of being "in love" with the divine or with our lover, spouse, job, artistic idol, car, and so on, all the while forgetting that we, in fact, are not only in love but are love itself. We look outward for love, yet if we begin to truly look in the way that Kabir suggests, our attention begins to turn inward. We can cultivate and nourish a more discerning introspection through meditation or devotional practice. And as our attention sharpens through this inner reflection, the fog of our mind clears, and the cloud of confusion about our identity dissipates. Eventually, with consistent and sincere *looking*, the seeming edges of our little drops in the ocean yield to the realization of pure love. We find that the journey to love is through love.

It takes courage to fearlessly accept love and its power to transform us. Yet, as we do, we steadily become an expression of love and its companions: acceptance, joy, patience, compassion, and gratitude. Our words and actions become an extension of the grace and abundance of love. We realize that our true nature is to be free of the constraints we have created, often unwittingly, with the weight of our experiences.

In an effort to share the story of pure love through poetic voice, in this collection we link the words of poets, songwriters, and playwrights as well as quotes from holy books, lyrics of folk songs and operas, all from a diversity of genres, cultures, and time periods. These works are all a tribute to pure, boundless love.

The diverse voices form a mala, or a garland of 108 prayer beads. Although identified with Eastern traditions, the mala has been increasingly accepted as a sacred tool in other parts of the world. All the beads of a mala are equal, complete in themselves, and yet related to one another. Each turning of the beads steadies and deepens a connection to the Supreme. On a practical level, this collection — like the mala — is an interactive tool allowing the reader to commune with love. We can read the poems aloud in the same way we might recite a mantra or a prayer with a mala. Consistent use helps foster a shift in our neural pathways, so that eventually we *become* that which we meditate on. We become love.

At the highest level, the number 108 refers to Allah, the Divine, God, the Beloved, the Great Spirit, the Light, or the Ultimate Truth. In mathematics and science we find numerous references to the number 108. It is a multiple of the essential numbers two, three, and four as well as a product of the powers of one, two, and three. Astrologically, the combination of the nine planets and twelve signs of the sun of the zodiac is 108. In honor of the sacredness of this number, we have organized the book so that there are twelve poems within the nine sections, or phases of the sun's passage: from dawn through high noon to dusk, to moonlight, and then into the infinite stillness of the night.

This metaphor reflects the cycle of love from its initial urges until it quietly arrives home in the self-realization of pure love. Some readers may prefer an alternative metaphor: that the fiery essence of love arises from a faint spark into flames of passion and romantic love before fading into embers and settling with devotion into transcendental stillness. The poems express this evolution from a love that has an object to one that is all encompassing. Guiding this metaphor is the philosophical exploration of the role of love in moving through dualism into nondualism.

When we are absorbed in pure love, we see the world with childlike eyes, free of judgment. We notice the beauty in the ordinary, such as the way sun awakens the morning and the dew rests on a blade of grass. Everything seems to effortlessly pulse, just like the beating of our heart. We feel in sync with the change of seasons, the movement of the tides, and the patterns of the moon.

It is our wish that by reading and rereading this collection, you will be guided to that place of deep peace and balance and that you will fulfill your highest aspirations on your spiritual path to love.

Dawn

The heart has its reasons which
Reason knows nothing of.

BLAISE PASCAL

This

Sky

Where we live

Is no place to lose your wings

So love, love,

Love.

HAFIZ

Translated by Daniel Ladinsky

It is there
that our hearts are set,
In the expanse
of the heavens.

ANONYMOUS (PAWNEE)

Translated by Frances Densmore

For everything there is a season, and
a time for every matter
under heaven:
a time to be born,
and a time to die…

BOOK OF ECCLESIASTES

And
yet one word
frees us of all the weight and pain of life:

That word is
love.

SOPHOCLES

Translated by Robert Fitzgerald

And love
Says,

"I will, I will take care of you,"

To everything that is
Near.

HAFIZ

Translated by Daniel Ladinsky

Night is passing,
sun comes by dawn,
Awaken now, beauty's essence,
heart of love.

HAKIM OMAR KHAYYÁM

Translated by Nahid Angha, PhD

All you need is love, love
Love is all you need.

JOHN LENNON and PAUL MCCARTNEY

The Angel that presided o'er my birth
Said 'Little creature, form'd of joy and mirth,
Go, love without the help of anything on earth.'

WILLIAM BLAKE

Even if I
repeated love's name
forever,
could outward life match
the intensity of our hearts?

Izumi Shikibu

Translated by Jane Hirshfield

Since I was cut from the reed bed
I have made
this crying sound. Anyone
separated from someone he loves
understands what I say:

> *Anyone pulled*
> *from a source*
> *longs to go back.*

RUMI

Translated by Coleman Barks

All my heart is lonely,
All my heart is full of sorrow.
My lover, my lover is departed.

Dark the sky at evening,
Sad the bird notes in the dawning.
My lover, my lover is departed.

He was all my sunshine,
His the beauty and the gladness.
Return, return, gladness and joy.

ANONYMOUS (CHIPPEWA)

Translated by Frances Densmore

Morning Rays

Come to me in the silence of the night;
  Come in the speaking silence of a dream;
Come with soft rounded cheeks and eyes as bright
  As sunlight on a stream;
    Come back in tears,
O memory, hope, love of finished years.

CHRISTINA G. ROSSETTI

Oh lift me from the grass!
I die! I faint! I fail!
Let thy love in kisses rain
On my lips and eyelids pale.
My cheek is cold and white, alas!
My heart beats loud and fast;—
Oh! press it to thine own again,
Where it will break at last.

PERCY BYSSHE SHELLEY

Dance me to your beauty
with a burning violin
Dance me through the panic
till I'm gathered safely in
Lift me like an olive branch
and be my homeward dove
Dance me to the end of love

LEONARD COHEN

Yes, until our last hours,
you will have me as your companion.
To shelter us, to shelter us together
the earth is wide, the earth is wide enough.
With you the affronts of destiny
I will firmly face,
as long as I feel your heart
beating over my heart. Yes.
Ah, yes! until our last hours.

VINCENZO BELLINI

Translated by William Weaver

Some day, if I should ever lose you,
will you be able then to go to sleep
without me softly whispering above you
like night air stirring in the linden tree?

RAINER MARIA RILKE

Translated by Albert Ernest Flemming

Who sculpted Love and
placed him over the fountain,
thinking that his fire
could be quenched with water?

ZENODOTUS

Translated by Shane Leslie

When you came, you were like red wine and honey,
And the taste of you burnt my mouth with its sweetness.
Now you are like morning bread,
Smooth and pleasant.
I hardly taste you at all for I know your savour,
But I am completely nourished.

AMY LOWELL

My belly, now, is as noble as my heart…
    And now I feel in my own breathing an
exhalation of flowers: all because of the one who
rests inside me gently, as the dew on the grass!

GABRIELA MISTRAL

Translated by Stephen Tapscott

The cicada cries out
Burning with love.
The firefly burns
With silent love.

ANONYMOUS

Translated by Kenneth Rexroth

Tranquil our paths
When your hand rests on mine in joy.

Your voice gives life, like nectar.

To see you, is more than food or drink.

ANONYMOUS

Translated by Ezra Pound and Noel Stock

O how big is my beloved,
More than all the ones I know.
O how lively does my heart beat,
When I only see him glow.
Love can never be forced;
Treat it fondly, it will grow!

ANONYMOUS (SWAHILI)

Touched by all that love is
I draw closer toward you
Saddened by all that love is
I run from you

Surprised by all that love is
I remain alert in stillness

František Halas

Noon

Not speaking of the way,
Not thinking of what comes after,
Not questioning name or fame,
Here, loving love,
You and I look at each other.

YOSANO AKIKO

Translated by Kenneth Rexroth

My bounty is as boundless as the sea,
My love as deep; the more I give to thee,
The more I have, for both are infinite.

WILLIAM SHAKESPEARE

My love has two lives, in order to love you:
that's why I love you when I do not love you,
and also why I love you when I do.

PABLO NERUDA

Translated by Stephen Tapscott

As with lovers:
When it's right, you can't say
Who is kissing whom.

GREGORY ORR

I couldn't tell fact from fiction
      or if my dream was true,
The only sure prediction
      in this whole world was you.
I'd touched your features inchly,
      heard love and dared the cost.
The scented spiel reeled me unreal
      and found my senses lost.

MAYA ANGELOU

I gave my first love laughter,
　　I gave my second tears,
I gave my third love silence
　　Through all the years.

My first love gave me singing,
　　My second eyes to see,
But oh, it was my third love
　　Who gave my soul to me.

SARA TEASDALE

No fire
nor coals
could burn as hotly
as the secret love
which no one knows.

FOLK SONG

I choose your love
above all else. As for wealth
if that comes, or goes, so be it.
Wealth and love inhabit separate worlds.

But as long as you live here inside me,
I cannot say that I'm suffering.

SANAI

Translated by Coleman Barks

This is how I would die
into the love
I have for you:
As pieces of cloud
dissolve
in
sunlight.

RUMI

Translated by Coleman Barks

I greet what I love
With my heart's blood
And my senses wither
In love's fury

HADEWIJCH

Translated by Oliver Davies

One needs a friend on the path of love,
  An illumination, an intention.
On the way of love, one must become the dust
  Under the footfalls of the guide, a nothing blended
with the light of being.

MOULANA SHAH MAGHSOUD

Translated by Nahid Angha, PhD

The minute I heard my first love story
I started looking for you, not knowing
how blind that was.

Lovers don't finally meet somewhere.
They're in each other all along.

RUMI

Translated by Coleman Barks

Dappled Afternoon

Oh, flaming lantern!
You illuminate the darkest pockets of my soul.
Where once I wallowed in bitter separation
now, with exquisite intensity,
I radiate warmth and light to my Beloved.

How peacefully, how lovingly
you awaken my heart,
that secret place where you alone dwell within me!
Your breath on my face is delicious,
calming and galvanizing at once.
How delicately, how lucidly
you make me crazy with love for you!

ST. JOHN OF THE CROSS

Translated by Mirabai Starr

In the flood of Thy love
I have rapture eternal
And prayer is but
an occasion for praise.

SOLOMON IBN GABIROL

Translated by Israel Zangwill

My Joy—
My Hunger—
My Shelter—
My Friend—
My Food for the Journey—
My Journey's End—
You are my breath,
My hope,
My companion,
My craving,
My abundant wealth.
Without You — my Life, my Love —
I would never have wandered across these endless
    countries.
You have poured out so much grace for me,
Done me so many favors, given me so many gifts—
I look everywhere for Your love—
Then suddenly I am filled with it.

RĀBIʿA

Translated by Charles Upton

Only

That Illumined
One

Who keeps
Seducing the formless into form

Had the charm to win my
Heart.

Only a Perfect One

Who is always
Laughing at the word
Two

Can make you know

Of

Love.

HAFIZ

Translated by Daniel Ladinsky

He plays your name
to call you on his sweet reed flute.
He cherishes breeze-blown pollen
that touched your fragile body.
In woods on the wind-swept Jumna bank,
Krishna waits in wildflower garlands.

JAYDEVA

Translated by Barbara Stoler Miller

To the bridge of love,
old stone between tall cliffs
 — eternal meeting place, red evening —,
I come with my heart.
 — My beloved is only water,
that always passes away, and does not deceive,
that always passes away, and does not change,
that always passes away, and does not end.

JUAN RAMÓN JIMÉNEZ

Translated by James Wright

With Thy look of love
Thou didst
Leave in me
grace and beauty.

St. John of the Cross

Translated by Edgar Allison Peers

That vague sweetness made my heart
ache with longing and it seemed to me
that it was the eager breath of summer
seeking for its completion.

I knew not then that it was so near,
that it was mine,
and that this perfect sweetness had
blossomed in the depth of my own heart.

RABINDRANATH TAGORE

A day so happy.
Fog lifted early, I worked in the garden.
Hummingbirds were stopping over honeysuckle
    flowers.
There was no thing on earth I wanted to possess.
I knew no one worth my envying him.
Whatever evil I had suffered, I forgot.
To think that once I was the same man did not
    embarrass me.
In my body I felt no pain.
When straightening up, I saw the blue sea and sails.

CZESLAW MIŁOSZ

The time will come
when, with elation,
you will greet yourself arriving
at your own door, in your own mirror,
and each will smile at the other's welcome,

and say, sit here. Eat.
You will love again the stranger who was your self.
Give wine. Give bread. Give back your heart
to itself, to the stranger who has loved you

all your life, whom you ignored
for another, who knows you by heart.

Derek Walcott

To wake at dawn with a winged heart
and give thanks for another day of loving;

To rest at the noon hour and meditate
love's ecstasy;

To return home at eventide with gratitude;

And then to sleep with a prayer for the
beloved in your heart and a song of praise
upon your lips.

KAHLIL GIBRAN

While the rose said to the sun,
"I shall ever remember thee,"
her petals fell to the dust.

RABINDRANATH TAGORE

Dusk

Hark to the unstruck bells and drums!
  Take your delight in love!
Rains pour down without water, and
  the rivers are streams of light.
One Love it is that pervades the whole
  world, few there are who know it fully:
They are blind who hope to see it by
  the light of reason, that reason
  which is the cause of separation —
The House of Reason is very far away!

KABIR

Translated by Rabindranath Tagore

The Ocean of Love

is a sea

where there is no shore;

And without the soul's surrender,

there is no hope,

no sand.

HAFIZ

Translated by T. R. Crowe

And God said to the soul:
  I desired you before the world began.
  I desire you now
  As you desire me.
  And where the desires of two come together
  There love is perfected.

MECHTHILD OF MAGDEBURG

Translated by Oliver Davies

I can give not what men call love,
     But wilt thou accept not
The worship the heart lifts above
     And the Heavens reject not, —
The desire of the moth for the star,
     Of the night for the morrow,
The devotion to something afar
     From the sphere of our sorrow?

Percy Bysshe Shelley

I have learned not to worry about love;
but to honor its coming
with all my heart.
To examine the dark mysteries
of the blood
with headless heed and
swirl,
to know the rush of feelings
swift and flowing
as water.
The source appears to be
some inexhaustible
spring
within our twin and triple
selves;
the new face I turn up
to you
no one else on earth
has ever
seen.

ALICE WALKER

True love gives us beauty, freshness,
solidity, freedom, and peace.

True love includes a feeling of
deep joy that we are alive.

THICH NHAT HANH

How long will you
keep pounding on an open door
Begging for someone
to open it?

RĀBI‘A

Translated by Charles Upton

Love is patient and kind;
love is not jealous or boastful;
it is not arrogant or rude.

Love does not insist on its own way;
it is not irritable or resentful;
it does not rejoice at wrong,
but rejoices in the right.

Love bears all things,
believes all things,
hopes all things,
endures all things.

Love never ends...

PAUL THE APOSTLE

What

Is the

Root of all these

Words?

One thing: love.

But a love so deep and sweet

It needed to express itself

With scents, sounds, colors

That never before

Existed.

HAFIZ

Translated by Daniel Ladinsky

Leave the window open.
I want to see who is coming.
How can they bury in a grave
someone who died from love?

ANONYMOUS (AZERBAIJANI)

Translated by Reza Baraheni and Zahra-Soltan Shokoohtaezeh

The gold moth did not love him
So, gorgeous, she flew away.
But the gray moth circled the flame
    Until the break of day.
And then, with wings like a dead desire,
She fell, fire-caught, into the flame.

LANGSTON HUGHES

Let this be
my last word,
that I trust in
Your love.

RABINDRANATH TAGORE

Starlit Eve

O God,
the stars are shining:
All eyes have closed in sleep:
The kings have locked their doors.
Each lover is alone, in secret,
with the one he loves.
And I am here too:
alone, hidden from all of them—
With You.

RĀBIʿA

Translated by Charles Upton

How sweet it is to love,
and to be dissolved,
and, as it were,
to bathe myself
in Thy love.

THOMAS À KEMPIS

Listen to the melodious music
of the divine poet.

He plays upon the flute of love,
the notes soar to the high heaven
and reach the distant stars
and dance on the raging waves of the sea.

THE VEDAS

I will utter your name, sitting alone among the shadows
of my silent thoughts.

I will utter it without words, I will utter it without
purpose.
For I am like a child that calls its mother a hundred
times, glad that it can say, "Mother."

RABINDRANATH TAGORE

I would liken you
To a night without stars
Were it not for your eyes.
I would liken you
To a sleep without dreams
Were it not for your songs.

LANGSTON HUGHES

I love you without knowing how, or when, or from
    where.
I love you straightforwardly, without complexities
    or pride;
so I love you because I know no other way

than this: where *I* does not exist, nor *you*,
so close that your hand on my chest is my hand,
so close that your eyes close as I fall asleep.

PABLO NERUDA

Translated by Stephen Tapscott

I am wild, I will sing to the trees,
   I will sing to the stars in the sky,
I love, I am loved, he is mine,
   Now at last I can die!

I am sandaled with wind and with flame,
   I have heart-fire and singing to give,
I can tread on the grass or the stars,
   Now at last I can live!

SARA TEASDALE

This moment this love comes to rest in me,
many beings in one being.
In one wheat-grain a thousand sheaf stacks.
Inside the needle's eye, a turning night of stars.

RUMI

Translated by Coleman Barks

The night has a thousand eyes,
    And the day but one;
Yet the light of the bright world dies
    With the dying sun.

The mind has a thousand eyes,
    And the heart but one;
Yet the light of a whole life dies
    When love is done.

FRANCIS WILLIAM BOURDILLON

Everything makes love with silence.

They promised me a silence
like fire, a house of silence.

Suddenly the temple is a circus
the light a drum.

ALEJANDRA PIZARNIK

Translated by Susan Bassnett

As you fill with wisdom,
and your heart with love,
there's no more thirst.

There's only an unselfed patience
waiting on the doorsill, a silence
which doesn't listen to advice
from people passing on the street.

SANAI

Translated by Coleman Barks

I am the Mother
of fair love…
and of knowledge,
and of holy hope.
In me is all grace
of the way and of the truth…
My memory is
unto everlasting generations.

BOOK OF ECCLESIASTICUS

Moonlit Night

On the straying moonbeams
I shall steal over your bed,
and lie upon your bosom
while you sleep.
I shall become a dream,
and through the little opening of your eyelids
I shall slip into the depths of your sleep;
and when you wake up
and look round startled,
like a twinkling firefly
I shall flit out
into the darkness.

RABINDRANATH TAGORE

Oh come with me by moonlight, love,
And let us seek the river's shore;
My light canoe awaits thee, love,
The sweetest burden e'er it bore!

JOHN ROLLIN RIDGE

i carry your heart with me(i carry it in
my heart)i am never without it(anywhere
i go you go,my dear;and whatever is done
by only me is your doing,my darling)
                                        i fear
no fate(for you are my fate,my sweet)i want
no world(for beautiful you are my world,my true)
and it's you are whatever a moon has always meant
and whatever a sun will always sing is you

here is the deepest secret nobody knows
(here is the root of the root and the bud of the bud
and the sky of the sky of a tree called life;which grows
higher than soul can hope or mind can hide)
and this is the wonder that's keeping the stars apart

i carry your heart(i carry it in my heart)

E. E. CUMMINGS

Clear full moon,
The night is very still.
My heart sounds
Like a bell.

FOLK SONG

Translated by Kenneth Rexroth

You are the sky and the ground.
You alone the day, the night air.

You are the meal that's being brought,
the sandal knot, flowers and their watering.

You are all this.
What could I possibly bring You!

LALLA

Translated by Coleman Barks

I am filled with you.
Skin, blood, bone, brain, and soul.
There's no room for lack of trust, or trust.
Nothing in this existence but that existence.

RUMI

Translated by Coleman Barks

I am

A hole in a flute

That the Christ's breath moves through—

Listen to this

Music.

I am the concert

From the mouth of every

Creature

Singing with the myriad

Chords.

HAFIZ

Translated by Daniel Ladinsky

I am the One whom I love, and the One whom I love is
    myself.
We are two souls incarnated in one body;
if you see me, you see Him,
if you see Him, you see us.

MANSUR AL-HALLAJ

Translated by Bernard Lewis

I am a fountain, You are my water.
I flow from You to You.

I am an eye, You are my light,
I look from You to You.

You are neither my right nor my left.
You are my foot and my arm as well.

I am a traveler, You are my road.
I go from You to You.

ZEYNEP HATUN

The beloved is you.

Shahram Shiva

We were parted
many thousands of eons ago,
yet we have not been
separated even for a moment.
We are facing each other
all day long,
yet we have never met.

ANONYMOUS (ZEN)

Midnight. No waves,
no wind, the empty boat
is flooded with moonlight.

DŌGEN ZENJI

Stillness

It was late, late in the evening,
    The lovers they were gone;
The clocks had ceased their chiming,
    And the deep river ran on.

W. H. AUDEN

A vessel of Wine, a book of Love
A loaf of bread, and passing of the time
And You and I are in the ruins
A feast beyond the dream of a king.

HAKIM OMAR KHAYYÁM

Translated by Nahid Angha, PhD

The traveller has to knock
at every alien door to come to his own,
and one has to wander through all the outer worlds
to reach the innermost shrine at the end.

My eyes strayed far and wide before
I shut them and said, "Here art thou!"

The question and the cry, "Oh, where?"
melt into tears of a thousand streams
and deluge the world with the flood of
assurance, "I am!"

RABINDRANATH TAGORE

On a dark night,
Inflamed by love-longing—
O exquisite risk!—
Undetected
I slipped away.
My house, at last,
grown still.

ST. JOHN OF THE CROSS

Translated by Mirabai Starr

But love of God
hath so absorbed me
that neither love
nor hate
of any other thing
remains in my heart.

Rābiʿa

I know nothing, I understand nothing,
I am unaware of myself.
I am in love, but with whom I do not know.
My heart is at the same time
both full and empty of love.

'ATTĀR

Translated by C. S. Nott

losing its name
a river
enters the sea

JOHN SANDBACH

Wild Nights — Wild Nights!
Were I with thee
Wild Nights should be
Our luxury!

Futile — the Winds —
To a Heart in port —
Done with the Compass —
Done with the Chart!

Rowing in Eden —
Ah, the Sea!
Might I but moor — Tonight —
In Thee!

EMILY DICKINSON

I have lived and I have loved;
I have waked and I have slept;
I have sung and I have danced;
I have smiled and I have wept;
I have won and wasted treasure;
I have had my fill of pleasure;
And all these things were weariness,
And some of them were dreariness.
And all these things — but two things
Were emptiness and pain:
And Love — it was the best of them;
And Sleep — worth all the rest of them.

CHARLES MACKAY

Whatever happens. Whatever
what is is is what
I want. Only that. But that.

GALWAY KINNELL

There's a tree that existed before the woods,
in age twice as old.
Its roots suffered as the valley changed,
its leaves deformed by wind and frost.
People all laugh at its withered aspect,
caring nothing about the core's beauty.
When the bark is all stripped off,
only essence remains.

HANSHAN

Translated by Tony Barnstone

The clear bead at the center
changes everything.
There are no edges
to my loving now.

RUMI

Translated by Coleman Barks

Eternity

The reeds give
way to the

wind and give
the wind away

A. R. AMMONS

Then there
crept
A little noiseless noise
among the leaves,
Born of the very sigh
that silence heaves.

JOHN KEATS

Silence, unmoved and rising,
Silence, unmoved and sheltering,
Silence, unmoved and permanent,
Silence, unmoved and brilliant,
Silence, broad and immense like the Gaṅgā,
Silence, unmoved and increasing,
Silence, white and shining like the Moon,
Silence, the Essence of Śiva.

CIVAVĀKKIYAR

Sitting over words
very late I have heard a kind of whispered sighing
not far
like a night wind in pines or like the sea in the dark
the echo of everything that has ever
been spoken
still spinning its one syllable
between the earth and silence

W. S. MERWIN

Come quickly — as soon as
these blossoms open,
they fall.
This world exists
as a sheen of dew on flowers.

Izumi Shikibu

Translated by Jane Hirshfield

A great dark sleep
Has fallen on my life:
Sleep, all hope,
Sleep, all want!

I see nothing any more.
I have lost memory
Of good and of bad...
O the sad story!

I am a cradle
Rocked by a hand
In the hollow of a crypt:
Silence, silence!

PAUL VERLAINE

Translated by Kate Flores

Silently a flower blooms,
In silence it falls away;
Yet here now, at this moment, at this place,
    the whole of the flower, the whole of the world is
    blooming.
This is the talk of the flower, the truth of the blossom;
The glory of eternal life is fully shining here.

ZENKEI SHIBAYAMA

Translated by Sumiko Kudo

As the flowing rivers
in the ocean
Disappear,
quitting name and form,
So the knower,
being liberated
from name and form,
Goes unto the heavenly Person,
higher than the high.

THE UPANISHADS

Translated by Robert Ernest Hume

The birds have vanished down the sky.
Now the last cloud drains away.

We sit together, the mountain and me,
until only the mountain remains.

LI PO

Translated by Sam Hamill

I saw myself when I shut my eyes:
space, space
where I am and am not.

OCTAVIO PAZ

Translated by Muriel Rukeyser

The lamp once out:
Cool stars enter
The window frame.

NATSUME SŌSEKI

Translated by Sōiku Shigematsu

That

which by knowing

everything is known.

THE UPANISHADS

AUTHORS AND POETS

YOSANO AKIKO (Shō Hō) (1878–1942) was a prolific writer. She came from a respected merchant family and at age eleven was responsible for the family's business. Later on, while raising thirteen children, she actively championed feminism, pacifism, and social reform in Japan. Known for her poetry expressing female beauty and sensuousness, she authored more than seventy-five books.

A. R. AMMONS (Archie Randolph) (1926–2001) grew up on a tobacco farm in North Carolina and began writing poetry while in the military service. Ammons became a distinguished professor and an award-winning poet, receiving multiple honors during his lifetime. A major theme in his poetry is humanity's relationship to the natural world.

MAYA ANGELOU (1928–2014) was born as Marguerite Johnson in St. Louis and raised mostly by her grandmother, who modeled faith, courage, and love, values that stayed with Angelou for life. She went on to become one of the most influential and honored voices of our time, with more than fifty honorary doctorate degrees and dozens of awards, including the Presidential Medal of Freedom.

'ATTĀR (Attar of Nishapur; Abū Ḥamīd bin Abū Bakr Ibrāhīm) (c. 1110–1221) was a Persian Muslim poet born in Nishapur. As a young man he worked at a pharmacy, where his customers confided in him, an experience that affected him deeply. Eventually he abandoned the pharmacy and traveled widely, returning home to promote Sufism.

W. H. AUDEN (1907–1973), born in York, England, is considered the greatest Anglo-American poet of the twentieth century. Encyclopedic in scope and technical achievement, his four hundred poems elucidate everything from pop cliché to profound meditation. Awarded the Pulitzer Prize in 1948, Auden also composed hundreds of essays, lectures, and reviews, whose power gave him the status of respected elder statesman.

VINCENZO BELLINI (Vincenzo Salvatore Carmelo Francesco Catania Bellini) (1801–1835) was the first of seven children born to a musical family in Catania, Sicily. According to legend, he sang an aria at eighteen months, began studying music theory at age two, had his first piano lessons at three, played piano to an audience at five, and composed his first pieces at age six. Young Bellini's compositions were heard in churches and in the salons of the aristocracy, and he became a famous opera composer known for his long-flowing melodic lines.

WILLIAM BLAKE (1757–1827) was born in London and at an early age had visions of angels, the Virgin Mary, and historical figures, visions said to have influenced him throughout his life. Blake wrote his first poetry at the age of twelve. As a poet, painter, and engraver, he challenged conventional values and views and was widely misunderstood. After his death, his critics came to recognize him for his expressiveness and creativity and for the mystical undercurrents of his work.

FRANCIS WILLIAM BOURDILLON (1852–1921) was a poet and translator. Little is known about his early life other than that he grew up near Midhurst, Sussex, where he later returned to build a home. In addition to writing, he served as a tutor to the sons of Prince Christian of Schleswig-Holstein and at the University of Eastbourne.

CIVAVĀKKIYAR (c. ninth century) was a Tamil siddha, or one who understood liberation and experienced divine light and power from within. Though his life story is unknown, his poetry reveals that he was a great mystic and poet. Civavākkiyar is viewed as a forthright rebel who ignored divisions in society and faiths.

LEONARD COHEN (1934–), singer, songwriter, musician, painter, poet, and novelist, was born in Montreal. His father was the son of a Polish immigrant and died when Cohen was nine, and his mother was the daughter of a rabbi of Lithuanian ancestry. Cohen is one of the most influential singer-songwriters from the sixties, and his career and impact reach into the twenty-first century. His numerous awards include a Grammy Award for Lifetime Achievement in 2010 and a 2012 PEN Award for Song Lyrics of Literary Excellence.

E. E. CUMMINGS (Edward Estlin) (1894–1962) grew up in a Unitarian household in Cambridge, Massachusetts, with a father who was a minister and professor and a mother who loved language. During World War I, Cummings volunteered for the ambulance corps and was imprisoned for several months in France on suspicion of treason. Themes in his poetry include love and nature and the relationship of the individual to the world. At the time of his death, Cummings was the second most widely read poet, after Robert Frost.

EMILY DICKINSON (1830–1886) lived most of her life on the family property in Amherst, Massachusetts. She published only a dozen poems during her lifetime, achieving fame only after her death, when her cache of almost 1,800 poems was discovered and the breadth of her work became apparent. Themes of death and immortality pervade her poems and her numerous letters to her friends and family.

KAHLIL GIBRAN (1883–1931) was an artist and poet, born in the town of Bsharri, in Mount Lebanon. Because of his family's poverty, he received no formal schooling during his childhood, except for the priests who used to visit him to instruct him in the Bible. As a young man he immigrated to the United States, where he began to write, in both English and Arabic. Gibran is best known for his book *The Prophet*, which consists of twenty-six poetic essays and was one of the bestselling books in the twentieth century in the United States.

HADEWIJCH (Hadewijch of Brabant) (c. early thirteenth century) was a Flemish poet and mystic, probably born in the Duchy of Brabant. She was thought to have come from a noble family because of her extensive knowledge of literature and theology in other languages. Her writings include poems, letters, and descriptions of her visions.

HAFIZ, or HAFEZ (Khwāja Shams-ud-Dīn Muhammad Hāfez-e Shīrāzī) (c. 1320–1389), was a great Persian Sufi whose poetry expresses longing and love for the divine. It is said that after his father died, Hafiz took work at a bakery, where he saw a girl whose beauty inspired him to win her love. During a forty-night vigil, he had a vision of an angel that led to his realization that God was infinitely more beautiful than any human form. The angel revealed where Hafiz could find his spiritual master, Attar of Shiraz, who subsequently led Hafiz to union with God.

FRANTIŠEK HALAS (1901–1949), Czech poet, essayist, and translator, came from a family of textile workers and was raised by his grandmother while his father served in the Czech Legion. After finishing his formal education in his midteens, Halas continued to learn in his job as a bookseller. During World War II he took part in the resistance movement, and his works are a complex interweaving of the upheavals of the war and his views of the individual and society.

MANSUR AL-HALLAJ (Abū 'l-Muġīṭ Al-Ḥusayn bin Manṣūr al-Ḥallāğ) (c. 858–922), born in Persia, was the son of a *hallaj*, a cotton and wool carder, and at an early age had the Qur'an memorized. He began his wanderings at eighteen and traveled as widely as China and India, openly sharing utterances and his teachings with the masses. It is said that when he was executed, for heresy, even his ashes cried, "I am the Truth." An archetypal model of the intoxicated lover of God, he was one of the first Sufi masters.

THICH NHAT HANH (Nguyenn Xuan Bảo) (1926–) entered a monastery at age sixteen and was ordained as a monk in 1949. He has become a global spiritual leader, poet, and peace activist, revered around the world for his powerful teachings and writings on mindfulness and peace. Born in Vietnam, he lives in Plum Village in the south of France.

HANSHAN (Hánshān, meaning "Cold Mountain"; Kanzan in Japanese) (fl. ninth century) is the name given to the Tang dynasty author of a collection of poems in the Taoist and Zen traditions. His poems often reflect his life of hermitage at Cold Mountain and many have been noted for their straightforwardness, unusual for that time. Hanshan is honored in the Buddhist tradition as an emanation of the bodhisattva Mañjuśrī.

ZEYNEP HATUN (?–1474) was one of the first female Sufi poets of the Ottoman Empire. Though little is known about her life, two of her contemporaries, the poets Latifi and Aşık Çelebi, mention that she spent part of her life in Istanbul, and Çelebi writes that she was an activist for women's position in society.

LANGSTON HUGHES (1902–1967) was raised mostly in Lawrence, Kansas, by his maternal grandmother, who was one of the first women to attend Oberlin College, and his grandfather, who was an educator and activist for the rights of African Americans. Hughes eventually moved to Illinois to reunite with his mother, who had been working to support the family. He wrote his first short stories, plays, and poems in high school and never stopped writing, authoring a large body of poetic work, as well as eleven plays and countless works of prose. He is perhaps best known as one of the leaders of the Harlem Renaissance.

SOLOMON IBN GABIROL (Hebrew, Solomon ben Yehuda; Latin, Avicebron) (c. 1021–c. 1058), born in Málaga, was famous by age sixteen for his religious hymns. An accomplished Neoplatonic philosopher, Gabirol wrote both sacred and secular poems in Hebrew during what is now known as the Jewish Golden Age in Spain.

JAYDEVA (c. twelfth century) was a poet-saint whose name is an epithet of Krishna. According to legend, he was born in East India to a Brahman family. At a young age he abandoned scholarship and became a wandering ascetic devoted to God. He then left his ascetic life to marry Padmāvatī, whose father convinced Jaydeva that the divine Jagannātha himself had ordained the marriage. Jaydeva expressed the intricacies of divine and human love in his lyrical poem *Gītagovinda*, which celebrates the love between Krishna and Radha.

JUAN RAMÓN JIMÉNEZ (1881–1958), a Spanish poet, lost his father in his late teens and was sent to France and then to a sanatorium in Madrid for help in overcoming his grief. Reportedly, in both places he had numerous love affairs, first with his doctor's wife and then with different nurses. With the onset of the Spanish Civil War, he and his wife, Zenobia, who was also a writer, went into exile and later settled in Puerto Rico. In 1956 Jiménez received the Nobel Prize in Literature.

JOHN OF THE CROSS, ST. (Juan de Yepes y Álvarez) (1542–1591), a Spanish mystic and writer, received his first formal education at a Jesuit school. In his twenties, he became a Carmelite friar and met St. Teresa of Avila. Their joint reform work led to his being imprisoned and tortured for nine months by his fellow priests. While in prison, St. John had a life-transforming realization of the veil that separates us from God. His axiom was that the soul must empty itself of self in order to be filled with God. After escaping prison, he lived a life of joyful solitude.

KABIR (Kabīr; often interpreted as "Guru's Grace") (1398–1448 or 1440–1518) was raised by a Muslim family of weavers in India. Legend has it that his birth mother was a Brahman widow. At an early age, Kabir became a disciple of the Hindu bhakti saint Ramananda. When Kabir died, it is said that his body turned to flowers and that his Hindu and Muslim followers each took half to perform last rites. As poet-saint in the bhakti and Sufi traditions, he expressed self-surrender, divine love, and an inward worship of the Beloved in his writings.

JOHN KEATS (1795–1821), one of the most beloved of the English Romantic poets, lost both of his parents by the age of fifteen and published his first poem at twenty-one. Though he received his apothecary's license, he decided to be a poet instead of a surgeon. In his short life he produced an enduring body of work, including the great epic poem *Endymion*.

HAKIM OMAR KHAYYÁM (Ghiyāth ad-Dīn Abu'l-Fath 'Umar ibn Ibrāhīm al-Khayyām Nīshāpūrī) (1048–1131) was born in Persia to a family of tent makers. He went on to be an accomplished scientist, philosopher, and poet and was best known as a mathematician and astronomer. Scholars debate whether he was a Sufi and also whether his work *Rubáiyát of Omar Khayyám* is a spiritual metaphor or a collection of sensual love poems.

GALWAY KINNELL (1927–2014) was raised in Pawtucket, Rhode Island, and was drawn to poetry at an early age by the musicality of the language. After traveling extensively in Europe and the Middle East, Kinnell became an advocate for a just and peaceful world. His writing concerns both social and spiritual issues and is filled with nature imagery. For his 1982 collection, *Selected Poems*, he won the Pulitzer Prize and shared the National Book Award with Charles Wright.

LALLA (Lal Diddi, Lalleswari, Lale'ded, Lal Ded) (1320–1392) was born in Kashmir and married at the age of twelve. After years of harsh treatment at the hands of her mother-in-law and her husband, Lalla left to live the life of a wandering devotee in the Shaivite tradition. Renouncing the world, she expressed her joyful union with her beloved Lord through song and dance. Her realizations as a saint-mystic appeal to people across cultural and religious barriers.

JOHN WINSTON ONO LENNON (1940–1980) and SIR JAMES PAUL MCCARTNEY (1942–), born and raised in Liverpool, were members of the Beatles, the most commercially successful band in the history of popular music. Together they wrote hundreds of beloved, innovative, and enduring songs. Unlike many songwriting partnerships, both Lennon and McCartney wrote words and music, collaborating closely while writing.

LI PO (Li Bai) (c. 701–762) was probably born in central Asia. When he was four, his family moved to Sichuan province, where he flourished in his studies and the martial arts. In his early twenties he began a life of wandering and writing, going on to become a prominent Tang dynasty poet. His poems are a rich reflection of the times and influenced both Ezra Pound and James Wright.

AMY LOWELL (1874–1925) was born in Brookline, Massachusetts, into an accomplished family. An avid reader, book collector, and traveler, at the age of twenty-eight she became a poet. By the time of her death two decades later, she had published volumes of poetry, a biography on Keats, literary criticisms, and more. Lowell posthumously received the Pulitzer Prize for Poetry in 1926.

CHARLES MACKAY (1814–1889) was a Scottish poet, journalist, editor, novelist, and songwriter. His father was a naval officer, and his mother died shortly after his birth. Mackay began his education in London and after studying language in Brussels and traveling to France, he returned to London as an Italian tutor and continued to write, becoming best known for his songs.

MOULANA SHAH MAGHSOUD (1916–1980), born in Iran, received spiritual guidance from his father, Hazrat Mir Ghotbeddin Mohammad, a revered Sufi and scholar. Shah Maghsoud studied law at the University of Tehran and over his lifetime cultivated his talent at poetry as well as his knowledge of science and philosophy. His daughter, Nahid Angha, PhD, is the sole translator of his writings.

MECHTHILD OF MAGDEBURG (c. 1207–c. 1282/1294) was born into a wealthy German family and at age twelve said that she saw "all things in God, and God in all things." In her early twenties she entered the Beguines sisterhood and led a life of simplicity, service, and prayer. Over fourteen years, she received mystical visions and the divine instruction to record these experiences. Mechthild's love poetry has been compared to that of the Sufi poets of the Middle East and the bhakti poets of India.

W. S. MERWIN (William Stanley) (1927–) was raised in New Jersey and Pennsylvania. His parents had tough upbringings: his mother was orphaned and later lost her first child, and his father, a minister, came from a violent and harsh household. At age five, Merwin wrote hymns for his father and went on to study poetry at the university. His writings reflect his involvement with the antiwar movement, Buddhist philosophy, and the preservation of the rain forests. His many honors include two Pulitzer Prizes.

CZESLAW MIŁOSZ (1911–2004), born in Poland, traveled with his mother during World War I, following his father's work as an engineer in the czar's army across Russia. At the end of the war they settled in Vilna, Poland. Miłosz published his first poems within a year of graduating from high school. He worked for the underground presses in Warsaw during World War II and lived mostly in Paris and the United States, where he eventually settled. Miłosz's writings were banned in Poland until after he was awarded the 1980 Nobel Prize in Literature.

GABRIELA MISTRAL (Lucila Godoy Alcayaga) (1889–1957) was born in Chile and raised in a small Andean village, where she finished her formal education before the age of twelve. She became known as a dedicated educator, intellectual, and advocate for peace, justice, and the environment. Mistral often celebrated love within relationships and with God. She received a number of visiting professorships and served as consul in different countries. In 1945 she received the Nobel Prize in Literature, the first Latin American to do so.

PABLO NERUDA (Ricardo Neftalí. Reyes Basoalto) (1904–1973) lost his mother shortly after his birth. A beloved Chilean poet, he was first published at thirteen and soon thereafter adopted the pen name Neruda in memory of Jan Neruda, a Czech poet. Over his lifetime he served as diplomat, writer, and poet and was both loved and persecuted for his work. Neruda received prestigious awards, including the 1971 Nobel Prize in Literature "for a poetry that with the action of an elemental force brings alive a continent's destiny and dreams."

GREGORY ORR (1947–) grew up in the rural Hudson Valley. He suffered early experiences with death, including his own near-death experience as an activist during the civil rights movement. Orr said of his work in a National Public Radio interview, "I believe in poetry as a way of surviving the emotional chaos, spiritual confusions, and traumatic events that come with being alive." Like the ancient poet-saints, Orr expresses the idea that we can only be known through knowing. His poetry collections have been translated into several languages, and he has received several distinguished fellowships and scholarships.

BLAISE PASCAL (1623–1662), a French mathematician and philosopher, lost his mother at a young age, and his father decided to educate his three children on his own. Young Pascal excelled in science and mathematics, and at age sixteen, he produced the first of his many contributions to mathematics, known as Pascal's theorem. Pascal's six-year respite from Catholicism (his "worldly period") ended when he had a vision. Shortly thereafter he wrote his first major literary work on religion. His most influential theological masterpiece was posthumously referred to as *Pensées*.

PAUL THE APOSTLE (Saulos Tarseus; Paulos) (c. 5–c. 67) was a native of Tarsus, the capital city in the Roman province of Cilicia (Turkey). He wrote that he was "a Hebrew born of Hebrews," a Pharisee, and one who advanced in Judaism beyond many of his peers. He converted to Christianity when he had a vision while on the road to Damascus.

OCTAVIO PAZ (1914–1998), Mexican poet, was the son and grand-son of political journalists. He abandoned his law studies to work at a school for the children of peasants and workers, an experi-ence that inspired the first of his long poems. In his twenties Paz founded and wrote for a literary journal, *Barandal*. After travel-ing to the West Coast of the United States, he entered the diplo-matic service. Among his many honors is the 1990 Nobel Prize in Literature.

ALEJANDRA PIZARNIK (1936–1972) was born in Argentina to Jewish immigrant parents, was raised in a Jewish community, and received her education in Spanish and Yiddish. At eighteen she began university studies in philosophy and letters but later dropped out. Pizarnik was also trained in painting but felt com-pelled to write poetry. She published her first poems at age nine-teen and went on to write numerous poetry collections before ending her life at age thirty-six.

RĀ-BI'A (Rābi'ah al-Baṣrī; Rabi'a means "fourth child") (717–801) was born into poverty in Iraq. It is said that after her parents died, she was stolen and sold into slavery. To ease her hardship, she spent her nights in prayer and meditation. Her master freed her when he observed her shrouded in a divine light during her devotions. Once free, she became an ascetic in the desert. Un-like other great saints and mystics, her teacher was God himself rather than a master. By the time of her death in her eighties, she was continually united with her Beloved.

JOHN ROLLIN RIDGE (Cherokee: Cheesquatalawny, "Yellow Bird") (1827–1867) was the son and grandson of signatories to the Treaty of New Echota, which ceded the Cherokee lands and eventually led to the Trail of Tears. He is considered the first Na-tive American novelist and also began publishing poems while he was in law school in Arkansas. In his work as a journalist and editor he advocated for the Cherokee region to join as a state of the Union.

RAINER MARIA RILKE (1875–1926) was born in Prague, and for the first five years of his life, Rilke's mother dressed him in girl's clothing as a way to recover her lost daughter. Rilke was poetically and artistically gifted, yet his parents sent him to a military academy, which he eventually left to study philosophy, art history, and literature. Rilke went on to become one of the greatest German-language poets. His lyrical poetry reveals his belief in the coexistence of the material and spiritual realms.

CHRISTINA G. ROSSETTI (1830–1894) was born in England, the youngest child in a gifted family. Her father was an Italian poet, and her mother was dedicated to cultivating her children's intellects through reading religious works and classics. The importance of faith in Rossetti's life was set in childhood, and nearly half of her poetic work is devotional, reflecting themes such as the temporariness of earthly love. She began writing and dating her poems in 1842 and continued to write and publish for the rest of her life.

RUMI (Jalāl ad-Dīn Muḥammad Rūmī) (1207–1273) was born in Persia and settled in Turkey at age eight with his family. Rumi succeeded his father's position as head of a dervish school and at age thirty-seven met the whirling dervish Shams al-Din, whose divine presence awakened Rumi's own love for the divine. Rumi abandoned his scholarly position and began writing poetry, using metaphors to express his experience of mystical union and his intense longing for the divine. Rumi reached across cultural and social boundaries, and it is said that his funeral was attended by Persians, Muslims, Jews, Christians, and Greeks.

SANAI (Hakim Abul-Majd Majdūd ibn Ādam Sanā'ī Ghaznavi) (1080–1131/1141) was a Persian poet, born in what is now Afghanistan. It is said that he abandoned his role as a court poet when a drunk helped him recognize his pointless role in creating poems in praise of the court's sultan. Sanai then began study with a Sufi master named Yusef Hamdani and later wrote the *Walled Garden of Truth*, the first Persian mystical epic of Sufism, a work that continues to be read and studied.

JOHN SANDBACH is a contemporary American haiku poet who frequently blogs about haiku. He has published collections in both Japan and the United States, including *Blue Amnesia*, his collection of four hundred haiku.

WILLIAM SHAKESPEARE (1564–1616), born in Stratford-upon-Avon, is considered the greatest writer in the English language. He wrote thirty-eight plays, 154 sonnets, two long narrative poems, and other verses, the authorship of which is uncertain. His plays have been translated into every major living language and are performed more often than those of any other playwright.

PERCY BYSSHE SHELLEY (1792–1822) grew up in the countryside and had an open mind and wide-ranging interests. At ten, he started boarding school, where his writing provided respite from the bullying he endured. Later, when Shelley was expelled from the university because of his atheism, his father appealed to him to disavow his beliefs. Shelley refused and opted to lead a tumultuous life expressing his social and political ideals. He is considered one of the greatest of the English Romantic poets.

ZENKEI SHIBAYAMA (1894–1974) was ordained as a Zen monk in 1908 and for twenty-five years was Zen master of the Nanzen-ji Zen Monastery in Kyoto. He was also a professor, the author of numerous works in Japanese, and the head abbot of the Nanzenji

Organization, overseeing some five hundred Rinzai Zen temples. His 1960s lecture tours influenced the growth and establishment of Zen in the United States.

IZUMI SHIKIBU (c. 974–1034) was born into an aristocratic family and was a court poet during the Heian period of Japan, writing works that combine romantic longing with Buddhist contemplation. She married twice and was the lover of two princes. Shikibu is a member of Thirty-Six Medieval Poetry Immortals, a group of Japanese poets considered exemplars of poetic ability.

SHAHRAM SHIVA was born in Persia and migrated to the United States in his mid teens. He is an award-winning translator and scholar of Rumi, the author of several books, and a performance poet as well as a recording artist and teacher of spirituality.

SOPHOCLES (c. 496–c. 405 BCE), born in Colonus to a wealthy family, was one of three ancient Greek tragedians whose plays survive. He won many competitions for his dramas and is said to have been athletically and musically talented.

NATSUME SŌSEKI (Natsume Kinnosuke; Sōseki means "stubborn") (1867–1916), a novelist, poet, and writer of fairy tales, was moved around in his early years and lost his mother and two brothers in his teens. Because his family disapproved of his interest in literature and writing, Sōseki entered the university to become an architect. At the encouragement of friends he changed majors, earned a degree in English, and was given a scholarship to study in England. After he returned to Japan, he taught and later devoted himself to writing. He is considered one of the greatest modern Japanese writers.

RABINDRANATH TAGORE (Rabīndranātha Thākura; Gurudev) (1861–1941) was born into a leading family in Calcutta. From an early age he preferred independent learning and exploration to formal education. His writing reflected his ardent nationalism and his humanistic belief in freedom. Among his many artistic contributions were liberating Bengali literature and music from traditional models and helping to sensitize the West to the subtleties and richness of Indian culture. He was the first non-European to be awarded the Nobel Prize in Literature, in 1913.

SARA TEASDALE (1884–1933) was the youngest child in a devout and established St. Louis family. Frail and prone to illnesses, she was pampered and homeschooled until she was well enough to go to school at age ten. At twenty-three, she published her first poetry collection. Four years later she published her second collection, which was praised for its romantic content and lyrical mastery. Her *Love Songs* won her a 1918 Pulitzer Prize.

THOMAS À KEMPIS (Thomas of Kempen) (1380–1471) was the son of a blacksmith and a schoolmistress. He was inspired to join a spiritual community early on, and after his schooling he joined the Monastery of St. Agnes, where his brother Jan was the prior. Even after being ordained as a priest, he preferred the quiet of his own room, where he could pray, meditate, write, study, and copy manuscripts and the Bible. He is thought to be the author of *The Imitation of Christ*, a well-known book on Christian devotion.

PAUL VERLAINE (1844–1896) was a French Symbolist poet. His mother, who had miscarried in her earlier pregnancies, was especially devoted to her son, who was prone to anger and emotional instability. Verlaine studied law but wanted only to write poetry, publishing his first sonnet at nineteen and a collection of poems three years later. His brief experience of being incarcerated for wounding someone with a gun inspired him to return to Catholicism, which in turn spurred some of his most outstanding poems.

DEREK WALCOTT (1930–), born in Santa Lucia, comes from an artistic family. His father, who was a watercolorist and a poet, died before Walcott was born. His mother loved the arts and taught in the town's Methodist school. Walcott trained as a painter, studied as a writer, and published his first poem at age fourteen. After college he moved to Trinidad and worked as a teacher and art critic. He has received many distinguished honors, including the Nobel Prize in Literature in 1992.

ALICE WALKER (1944–), born in Eatonton, Georgia, is one of the most prolific writers and revered activists of our time, defending the rights of all living beings. Her books have sold more than fifteen million copies and have been translated into more than two dozen languages. Her writings include novels, children's books, short story collections, essays, and poetry. Her honors include a 1983 Pulitzer Prize in Fiction.

DŌGEN ZENJI (also Dōgen Kigen, Eihei Dōgen, or Koso Joyo Daishi) (1200–1253) was the founder of the Japanese Soto school of Zen. His parents' deaths during his childhood gave him an early realization of the transient nature of life, which led him to study and then become ordained as a monk. When he was twenty-three he left for China and received dharma transmission from Caodung master Ju-ching. Five years later he returned to Japan and authored his second major work to promote the practice of zazen. He continued to teach and write throughout his life.

ZENODOTUS (Zenodotus of Ephesus) (fl. 280 BCE) was a Greek grammarian and literary scholar and the first superintendent of the Library at Alexandria. He was especially noted for producing the first critical edition of Homer.

SOURCES AND PERMISSION ACKNOWLEDGMENTS

———◇◇◇◇◇———

EVERY EFFORT HAS BEEN MADE to trace the copyright holders of poetry in this book. The editors apologize if any poetry or other material has been included without permission. Gratitude is due to the following for permission to include poems or extracts from poetry in copyright.

"It Stops Working" by Kabir, from the Penguin publication *Love Poems from God: Twelve Sacred Voices from the East and West*. Copyright © 2002 by Daniel Ladinsky and used with his permission.

"This Sky," "And Love Says," "Laughing at the Word," "What Is the Root?" and "A Hole in the Flute" by Hafiz, from the Penguin publication *The Gift: Poems by Hafiz*. Copyright © 1999 by Daniel Ladinsky and used with his permission.

"Our hearts are set" by Anonymous (Pawnee), from *Earth Always Endures: Native American Poems*, edited by Neil Phillip. Copyright © 1996 The Albion Press Ltd. Reproduced with permission of the publisher.

"Night is passing" by Hakim Omar Khayyám, from *Ecstasy: The World of Sufi Poetry and Prayer*. Copyright © 2007 by Nahid Angha, PhD. Excerpt reproduced with permission of Nahid Angha, PhD.

"All You Need Is Love," words and music by John Lennon and Paul McCartney, copyright © 1967 Sony/ATV Music Publishing LLC. Copyright renewed.

ABOUT THE EDITORS

RAVI NATHWANI, coeditor of *Mala of the Heart: 108 Sacred Poems*, was born in a business family in East Africa and raised in India in the Vaishnav Hindu tradition. Ravi created the new course Hindu Yoga & Buddhist Meditation and taught it at Tufts University from 1998 to 2014. He also taught at JFK University in California. Prior to teaching at the university level, Ravi was an entrepreneur and built and led numerous successful businesses. He lectures on a variety of Vedic studies and teaches Yoga teacher training workshops across the United States and Mexico. He leads satsangs and meditation groups and teaches the Bhagavad Gita, Yoga Sutras, Law of Karma, and Advaita Vedanta. Ravi has an MBA from Boston University and has lived in Mumbai, London, Boston, San Francisco, and Mexico.

KATE VOGT is coeditor of *Mala of the Heart: 108 Sacred Poems*, published in 2010 by New World Library. Raised on a farm in western Kansas, Kate has an innate connection with inner quiet and sense of the eternal and temporal. These themes continue to anchor her study and endeavors to help make ancient wisdom accessible to the everyday person. Kate draws from the comprehensive scope of Yoga philosophy, especially the Yoga Sutras, for her offerings and practical tips on the inward journey home. Her writings, teacher trainings, presentations, courses, and seminars include the following: Yoga and Indian Art, Silence Within the Sound, There Is No Place Like Om, Just Breathe, Knowing Nature, and Grandma's Garden of Universal Values. Kate has a BA in art history from the University of Washington and an MBA from Seattle University. She has traveled extensively and has lived in Sweden, Denmark, and Germany, as well as on both coasts and in the Great Plains of the United States.